Animal Attack!

Hunting with Polar Bears

By Maeve Sisk

Gareth Stevens Publishing

Please visit our website, www.garethstevens.com. For a free color catalog of all our high-quality books, call toll free 1-800-542-2595 or fax 1-877-542-2596.

Library of Congress Cataloging-in-Publication Data

Sisk, Maeve.
Hunting with polar bears / by Maeve Sisk.
p. cm. — (Animal attack!)
Includes index.
ISBN 978-1-4824-0527-9 (pbk.)
ISBN 978-1-4824-0529-3 (6-pack)
ISBN 978-1-4824-0526-2 (library binding)
1. Polar bear — Juvenile literature. 2. Tundra animals — Juvenile literature. I. Sisk, Maeve T. II. Title.
QL737.C27 S576 2014
599.786—dc23

First Edition

Published in 2014 by
Gareth Stevens Publishing
111 East 14th Street, Suite 349
New York, NY 10003

Designer: Katelyn E. Reynolds
Editor: Therese Shea

Photo credits: Cover, p. 1 (cover, pp. 1, 3–24 background image) Ron Erwin/All Canada Photos/Getty Images; cover, pp. 1, 3–24 (background graphic) pashabo/Shutterstock.com; cover, pp. 4–23 (splatter graphic) jgl247/Shutterstock.com; p. 4 Marques/Shutterstock.com; p. 5 (map) Olinchuk/Shutterstock.com; pp. 5 (main), 9, 11, 13, 17, 19 iStockphoto/Thinkstock.com; p. 6 gillmar/Shutterstock.com; p. 7 Nagel Photography/Shutterstock.com; p. 14 Antoine Beyeler/Shutterstock.com; p. 15 GeoStock/Photodisc/Getty Images; p. 18 Iakov Filimonov/Shutterstock.com; p. 21 pr2is/Shutterstock.com.

Printed in the United States of America

CPSIA compliance information: Batch #CW14GS: For further information contact Gareth Stevens, New York, New York at 1-800-542-2595.

CONTENTS

Words in the glossary appear in **bold** type the first time they are used in the text.

SNIFFING OUT DINNER

A polar bear lumbers across the snow-covered ice. It stops and sniffs the air. It smells something! The bear begins to explore the surface of the ice. It sees a hole. The huge creature sits down and waits.

After an hour, a little round head with whiskers pops up to take a breath. A seal! Before it can get away, the hungry polar bear's powerful **jaws** swoop in and . . . CHOMP! The mighty predator has its dinner.

Polar bears, the largest land predators, live only in the Arctic.

SO BIG, SO DEADLY

Polar bears have huge bodies. A polar bear can be more than 8 feet (2.4 m) long. And it can weigh more than 1,400 pounds (636 kg)! That means it needs to eat a lot. A polar bear has **adaptations** that help it hunt.

Polar bears have a long neck, so they can stay on land, stick their head into water, and grab their prey. They also have great senses of smell, sight, and hearing that they can use to locate prey.

A polar bear's long claws help it grip the ice.

FAT AND FUR

To keep warm in cold Arctic conditions, polar bears have two secret weapons: fat and fur. Polar bears may have a layer of fat up to 4 1/2 inches (11.4 cm) thick!

Polar bear fur is perhaps even more important. It **repels** water. That means these bears can spend a lot of time in freezing waters without getting too cold. Their fur also helps them blend in with snow and ice and hide from prey. It's not white, though. It's actually see-through!

Polar bears are the only bears considered to be sea **mammals**!

ICE-COLD HUNTER

Polar bears live along the shore. When there's ice covering the ocean, they head out to hunt. Polar bears spend about half their day looking for food. Their favorite ocean prey is the ringed seal. Ringed seals grow to be about 5 feet (1.5 m) long and 200 pounds (91 kg), so they provide a good meal for the bears.

When on land, polar bears eat birds, eggs, and even plants. These don't have enough fat in them to keep a polar bear healthy, though. That's why hunting on sea ice is so important.

Polar bears also eat bearded seals, walruses, and beluga whales.

BEAR-Y PATIENT

Polar bears use two methods of hunting. The first is finding a seal's breathing hole in the sea ice. The polar bear may smell the seal's **scent** near the hole. It just stays still and waits for the seal to come up. Then it grabs the seal with its teeth or smashes it with a giant paw.

Seals can hold their breath for a while, but they usually come up every 5 to 15 minutes. However, they make many breathing holes, so it's not that easy to catch them.

Fact Hunter

A seal may make 15 different breathing holes in the ice.

Polar bears wait near openings in the ice for seals to come up for a breath.

SEAL STALKER

The other polar bear hunting method is **stalking**. Seals get out of the water to rest, to dry off and warm up, and to give birth. If a polar bear spots a seal on land, it will crawl toward it slowly.

Seals on land usually lift their head every few minutes to look for danger. When the seal raises its head to look around, the polar bear stops moving. Its light fur blends in with the snow and ice.

If the polar bear gets within 20 feet (6 m) of the seal, it can leap onto it!

GOING WITH THE FLOE

Polar bears have to eat a lot to keep their layer of fat. They also have to hunt a lot because few of their hunts are successful.

Polar bears are always on the move. They lose weight as they walk from place to place or swim from one **ice floe** to another looking for food. Polar bears paddle with their front paws at speeds of about 6 miles (9.7 km) per hour. They use their back legs like a boat's **rudder** to change directions!

Fact Hunter

Scientists studied a polar bear that swam more than 400 miles (644 km) in 9 days!

Polar bears are excellent swimmers.

POLAR BEAR CUBS

After they **mate**, polar bear mothers eat a lot to get ready to have cubs. Some dig dens in snow or earth on land, while others stay on the sea ice, closer to food.

Polar bear cubs are born from November to January. The mother and her cubs stay in the den until March or April. The cubs, like all mammals, drink their mother's milk during that time. The mother doesn't have anything to eat at all! When she comes out, she's hungry and ready to hunt.

Fact Hunter

By the time a polar bear cub is 8 months old, it may weigh 100 pounds (45 kg)!

A polar bear mother starts feeding her cubs meat as soon as they leave the den for the first time. They stay with her for over 2 years learning how to hunt.

HEARTLESS HUNTER OR JUST HUNGRY?

Polar bears only have one predator to fear, and that's people. Although most people aren't allowed to hunt polar bears anymore, polar bears face other dangers.

Worldwide pollution has been linked to polar bear **diseases**. Human activity has caused **climate change** in the Arctic. Warmer weather means less sea ice forms each year. Without sea ice, these big bears can't get enough to eat. You might think that polar bears are fearsome predators, but they're just trying to survive like all wild animals.

Polar Bears by the Numbers

length	8 feet (2.4 m) or more; females a bit smaller
height	about 5 feet (1.5 m) at shoulder
weight	as much as 1,400 pounds (636 kg)
life span	usually up to 18 years in the wild
population	20,000 to 25,000

GLOSSARY

adaptation: a change in a type of animal that makes it better able to live in its surroundings

climate change: long-term change in Earth's climate, caused partly by human activities such as burning oil and natural gas

disease: illness

ice floe: a floating sheet of ice smaller than an ice field

jaw: one of the bones that hold the teeth and make up the mouth

mammal: a warm-blooded animal that has a backbone and hair, breathes air, and feeds milk to its young

mate: one of two animals that come together to make babies. Also, to come together to make babies.

repel: to keep away

rudder: the part on a boat or plane that helps steer

scent: a smell

stalk: to follow something secretly